DATE DUE			
APR 0 8 2002			

Man in the Universe

DISCARDED

NUMBER 17

BAMPTON LECTURES IN AMERICA

DELIVERED AT COLUMBIA UNIVERSITY 1964

Man in the Universe

FRED HOYLE

Columbia University Press
NEW YORK AND LONDON

Fred Hoyle, F.R.S., F.R.A.S., is Plumian Professor of
Theoretical Astronomy and Experimental Philosophy at
Cambridge University

Contents

Man in the Universe

Astronomy and Space Research

At first sight it is not easy to understand why so many astronomers are opposed to, or at least have doubts about, the space program. The simplest—and least analytical—explanation is that suggested by a popular British newspaper, which described the attitude of the Astronomer Royal and of myself as the inevitable reaction of old men to a new innovation. Possibly this may be a component in the way some of us feel, but it can only be a part of the story. It has in any case been easy for any astronomer who wished to hop on to the bandwagon to do so. The fact that many have not is interesting; and in this chapter I shall try to analyze reasons for hostility to the space program, with the hope that something more than merely destructive criticism will emerge.

I grew up in the years of the Depression. I was 14 years old when the economic catastrophe of 1929 struck down the whole of the technologically oriented parts of the world. Manifestly, my formative years were passed in an environment that must now be considered abnormal. As I recall it, there seemed two paths along which one might go in life. One was an endless, persistent quest of the apparently unobtainable, the holy grail of the age —money. The other was to regard economic prosperity as a bad joke, to stop worrying about wealth, to be satisfied with survival, but to insist on pursuing those activities in which one happened to be interested. I became a scientist because science was what I myself found interesting.

Nowadays, things are different. The broad mass of students attends universities and colleges in the frank pursuit of a meal ticket. Course work and examinations are ordeals to be endured to this end, in the fashion of initiation ceremonies. No doubt there are some students who wish to learn because they are deeply interested in their work, but the emphasis *in the average* has clearly changed. And the emphasis in science has also changed. We are much more conscious in our present-day science of its utility value than we were thirty years ago. Some cynics say that the main argument for the space program is its utility value, whether in the form of immediate technological "fall-out" or as an economic booster to a declining aircraft industry. The cynics are probably right. To the U.S. government, and to the State of California, the sputniks of October 1957 evidently came as a godsend.

Viewed in this light, the space program is far less objectionable than it is when presented as a species of astronomical crusade. During the Depression, it was Keynes,

I think, who first pointed out that the trouble with the economy was that it possessed positive feedback, that if governments artificially injected new terms of the correct sign into the body politic these would amplify themselves and the whole affair would soon develop galloping inflation. I do not think he described the situation quite as tersely as this, but he did make the important point that precise details of how the new terms were injected were irrelevant. Governments had to create jobs, to get things rolling, and it was irrelevant what jobs. I think Keynes actually made the point that it would be sufficient to dig large holes in the ground, and if nothing useful could be done with the holes it would be excellent to follow up the enterprise by filling them in again. So long as supporters of the space program take their stand on this argument, criticism loses much of its sting.

Before quitting the economic issue, however, there is an interesting question worth asking. What is the maximum scale of project that a nation should engage in? Suppose we divide national productivity into a specified number of units, say 1,000. How many units should we consume in our single largest technological project? Some elasticity is obviously required, depending on the strength of our value judgments. My own guess would be from 1 to 10 units. Since the space program fits into the upper part of this range, I do not think it comes outside what can be contemplated as a reasonable maximum, although it is most doubtful whether the purely scientific case would justify as much as the 1-unit level. My suspicion is that *relative to other projects* space research is now overweighted by a factor of at least 10. This consideration is relevant to our judgment because it is a critical point that if the biggest project is overweighted, if there is distortion at the top end of the scale, less expensive projects will inevitably suffer.

These considerations apply only to the one or two largest, wealthiest nations. Smaller nations would do well to set their maximum at a lower level, say at 1 unit of productivity. This is because the biggest projects (of which one can reasonably conceive) may turn out badly. It is the nature of a big project that it strains your resources. If it did not, then it would not cost so much. Confident statements are still being made about landing a man on the Moon and of retrieving him at a date around the year 1970. Because of these statements most people appear to take it for granted that the Moon project will succeed. It may. With a fair probability, I would suggest, it may not. A similar state of affairs will always apply to any nation which allows itself to go into a 1–10 unit project, the failure risk will always be quite high. Yet a big project for a small, or medium, nation is not a big project for a large nation. A 1-unit project for Britain is only an 0·1 unit project for the United States. If Britain engages in such a project it risks failure, but the United States on the same project would be certain to succeed. For this reason small nations should never engage in enterprises that stretch their resources, essentially because they will always be beaten by larger nations. So long as a small nation keeps well within its resources, however, it need experience no serious disadvantage. Only the very large nations can afford to go to the limit. There are many more small projects than large ones, so that objectively the small nation is not really at much disadvantage. Yet the opposite is usually asserted, and for a reason that is not far to seek. The big projects are the ones with strong emotional connections, the space program being no exception. With argument dominated by the lower brain centers, rather than by the cortex, small nations are apt to feel themselves out of the picture. And if they lose morale then of course they are.

About 95 percent of astronomical data is currently coming from ground-based equipment. In making this statement I am giving heavy weighting to the results, small in number but high in quality, that have come from satellite and rocket observations of X rays and γ rays. At least 50 percent of the data comes from ground-based optical telescopes. Without optical telescopes, data from radio-astronomy, from X rays, γ rays, would lose a half of its value, because it is the optical telescope that serves to identify the sources of these radiations. Most of the optical data comes from just six telescopes, the 60- and 100-inch telescopes on Mt. Wilson, the 200-inch telescope on Palomar Mt., the 82-inch Macdonald telescope, and the 120-inch telescope at the Lick Observatory. These instruments we owe in a large measure to the energy and determination of about half a dozen men, to George Ellery Hale for the 60- and 100-inch instru-

ments and for planning and raising the finance for the
200 inch, to Ira Bowen for establishing the 200 inch as a
working instrument, to Otto Struve for the 82 inch, and
to Donald Shane and Albert Whitford for the Lick instrument. Overwhelmingly, although not completely—
for the 120 inch stands to the credit of the University of
California—these projects were privately financed.
Next, a word about telescopes, particularly about their
use in making observations of faint, distant objects.

Start with 365 nights in the year, and then knock out
a good half, because the Moon makes the sky too bright
for observation of faint objects. Then knock out another
half because observing conditions are poor: cloud, atmospheric movements, dust in the air, and so on. So you
come down to about 80 usable nights a year. With these,
essentially, the whole load of modern extragalactic research has to be carried, chiefly on the only two modern
instruments among our six. Thus the 200 inch and the
120 inch give us a grand total of only 160 good nights a
year. This is the sum total of the present-day astronomical resource of the whole human species. You can easily
imagine that it does not go very far. To measure one red-
shift, of the most distant object so far known, Maarten
Schmidt took some 70 hours at the telescope. It needs no
deep logistic analysis to see that the bottleneck in modern astronomy lies in the acute shortage of high quality
optical telescopes *on the ground*.

Will this not be all changed as soon as satellite observ-
atories are in orbit? No it will not, and for reasons that

must be stated in order to correct misconceptions that have become widely disseminated and believed. When it was decided at government level to go ahead with the space program, a lot of good reasons for developing an orbiting observatory presented themselves. A telescope above the atmosphere would not be subject to the atmospheric troubles already noted above, in fact observing conditions should be better than anything which is experienced from the ground, even under the best conditions. Because ultraviolet light with wave lengths less than 3100 Å are absorbed in the atmosphere, a telescope in space would be capable of widening the "optical window." Third, the cost of an orbiting observatory is small compared to the over-all cost of the space program, so it would be absurd to go through with the space program but to forego an observatory in space.

These arguments are solid enough and nobody will begin to deny them. Unfortunately, however, the cart has been put before the horse. Instead of presenting the orbiting observatory as ancillary to the space program, the orbiting observatory has been offered as one of the important reasons for implementing the space program. As part of the campaign for selling the space program, the advantages of observation from space have been promulgated almost with Madison Avenue techniques. The key points in the logic of this sales technique run like this: You all know the wonderful discoveries that have been made with big telescopes, like those at Mt. Wilson and Palomar. O.K.? Now we have something that will make those big telescopes seem like a kid's spyglass. So, although its going to cost plenty, it'll be worth it.

The two objections to this argument are: first, it breaks the basic rule that nobody should attempt to advance his own projects by denigrating others; and, second, it has no contact with the facts. Competition for limited funds is one of the ugliest features of contemporary science. Unless energetic steps are taken to remove the causes of competition—in the sense of boosting oneself at somebody else's expense—it is inevitable that a serious malaise will develop. As regards the facts, one need only consult the best quality astronomical journals to realize that effectively the whole burden of observation still falls on the instruments to which I have already referred. This cannot be denied. It is usually met by a "wait-and-see" remark. Such a remark is impossible to argue against. All one can do is offer an opinion.

I believe telescopes in space will play an outstanding role in the astronomy of the future. But I think the time scale for parity in importance with ground-based equipment has been greatly misestimated. The extension into the ultraviolet has probably been exaggerated too, because absorption losses in the interstellar medium are likely to be worse than was expected at first. Some sprinkling of worthwhile results will probably appear in the next decade, but as an everyday working instrument the telescope in space may have to wait several decades. For a considerable while the gain over ground-based instruments will be less than has been claimed, because directional inaccuracies will to a considerable extent take the place of atmospheric seeing. This will be emphasized by ground-based equipment being constructed in particularly favorable sites, such as in Chile. So long as space techniques are based on chemical fuels, I suspect that ground-based equipment will not be superseded by equipment in space, although the latter must give some results that are not attainable from the ground. Generally speaking, projects in space should probably be viewed over a time scale of 50 years. There is not the slightest chance, I would say, of ground-based equipment being removed from the center of the stage on the time scale that is usually talked about in connection with the space program.

I hope that by now I have established the overwhelming case that exists for building many more ground-based telescopes, *if modern society is at all interested in astronomy*—if it is not, then for heaven's sake let us drop all the cant about astronomy from talk about the space program. Let us come back to our cost scale. The space program is consuming roughly 1 percent of the national product. How about telescopes? *Well, for only one-fifth of the space budget for 1 year it would be possible to build something like a hundred new 200-inch telescopes on the ground.*

As a theoretician, I have no personal stake in how money is spent on instruments, except in the sense that I am aware of how much my thoughts have been guided by what I have learned from different sources. Naturally, I want to see development occurring in those places from which I have learned most. And even those of you who are most remote from astronomy must frequently see pictures of remarkable astronomical objects. You can see them, almost from cover to cover in every issue of the *Scientific American*. Many commercial companies use them to their own ends, at no charge. Have you ever paused to reflect where those pictures were taken? Are you aware that the observatory most responsible for those pictures, most responsible for what we know about modern astronomy, recently applied to the wealthiest government agency for financial assistance to build a new telescope, a modest telescope costing about 0·0002 of the annual space budget, *and that the request was turned down?* Add to this that the observatory in question is the one where expertise in telescope construction everybody has relied on in the past twenty years and on which everybody plans to rely on in the future. Then I hope you will see something of the grotesque distortion, on the material side, that has been brought about, in part by crude envy and in part by the loss of a sense of value and judgment that has accompanied the acceleration of the space program. The chief danger in the space program lies in this loss of a sense of judgment; and the danger is perhaps worse on the abstract side than it is on the material side. In the rest of this chapter I shall be concerned with the abstract.

Anybody applying for a scientific research grant is

likely to come up against priorities of classification in which abstract questions come pretty low on the scale. The best project, from a point of view of securing substantial financial support, is a "useful project." A useful project is one that, if successful, will lead to the production of a large number of machines. It is more or less irrelevant what the machines are used for. They can indeed be quite pernicious, like the transistor radio. Yet I believe it is the abstract issues that are the really important ones. Destroy every machine on Earth, and within quite a short time our modern civilization would be reconstructed, due to the ideas we have in our heads. It is the way our brains work that is significant, not so much the machines. Of course, there is a sense in which the two go together. It is impossible for us to think the way we do without our being impelled to construct machines. But it is the ideas that are primary. Without ideas, know-how, without the understanding of the laws of physics, our machines would be just so much useless junk.

I think you will find from looking over the details of the grants of the National Science Foundation (and exactly the same of the grants made by the British S.R.C.) that substantially less than 10 percent goes into abstract research. My own perusal, admittedly only a sampling, gave about 2 percent. Well above 90 percent was gobbled up by machine projects. The usual explanation given for this curious situation is that equipment projects "cost more." Of course they do if you allow them to. A substantial reason for this lack of balance is that the merits of machine projects are easier to assess. If Einstein had put forward a project in 1910 for the development of relativity, how could a committee, the likes of which we operate with nowadays, have judged it? Perhaps, since it was Einstein, the project would have received support, although I am cynical about this. I once listened to $1 million being awarded in physics projects. Only two were turned down. They were from perhaps the two outstanding theoretical physicists in Britain. My protests, made quite strongly, did not receive the slightest support because the committee had on it certain "experts" who made it clear that they would take things ill if their judgments were overridden. This by the way is a grave objection to the committee system. Committee members are nearly always inhibited against offending each other. Yet it is probably correct that, if any enterprise is to go forward efficiently, decisions must be taken that offend many people. Just as natural selection depends on rejection and extinction, so successful enterprise depends on lots of offense being given.

Now that I am on the committee issue I find it difficult to let the subject drop. I recall once making what I believed to be a moving speech, to the effect that in assessing the relevant importance of different branches of science we must give priority to genuine advances in fundamental physics. I spoke warmly, and I believe well, but lost the critical vote. In the course of my harangue I was surprised to see one excellent scientist go literally and alarmingly very red in the face. Only afterward did I realize the truth, that many of the very best scientists in fields other than fundamental physics simply have not been able to face up to the concept that the laws of physics take pride of place in science. If instead of comparing the need for telescopes with the space program I was comparing telescopes with the need for an expensive accelerator I would be very torn in myself. So long as the accelerator people were not attempting to hog everything, I suspect that I would feel compelled to vote with them, even against the interests of astronomy. After this, however, I think the case for astronomy is overwhelmingly strong. Once we pass to the business of applying the laws of physics, as opposed to finding them, no subject compares with astronomy. In astronomy we have the lot. Find new physics today, and within two or three years it is likely that quite remarkable applications will occur in astronomy. Nonconservation of parity and the ensuing theories have played a critical role in our understanding of the later stages of stellar evolution. In the radio-galaxies, and in the newly discovered quasi-stellar sources, we are clearly entering the realm of high energy physics. Plainly, the Universe is a wider laboratory than anything which can be constructed here on Earth. Physics supplies us with the words, but it does not tell us how the words are to be put together to make up the play that we observe in the world around us. For this, we must look to astronomy on the large scale and to biology on the small scale.

I would like to come back to my main topic, stated at the outset, of why many astronomers have become skeptical about the space program. It will be clear that grounds exist for a reasonable measure of tactical objection. And by now the main strategical objection will also be clear. Nothing in the space program, except the X-ray and γ-ray work to which I have already referred, seems in any way related to the real aims of astronomy, which I take to be the interpretation of the play that constitutes the Universe. The X-ray and γ-ray observations, the astronomically most relevant part of the space program, are in any case ancillary to it and would almost certainly have happened without it. One cannot help wondering what is the relevance of a man being landed like a sack of potatoes on the Moon. Plainly, the relevance to astronomy is sensibly nil. As a feat of courage the enterprise ranks very high indeed. As a feat of physical skill it ranks lower than a good quarterbacking performance, or than the recent traverse of Mt. Everest, since electronic control must play a dominant role.

Should the space program go ahead? If the case for the space program rests on astronomical grounds, then quite certainly not. If the case is not astronomical, then astronomers have no real right to speak, not more than anybody else. But in that case astronomers cannot be considered in any way responsible if the project goes sour. What plainly needs to be done is to define the position. Today, NASA is so much engaged in astronomical matters that one cannot be blamed for taking astronomy to be at least an important façade in the space structure. Unless this façade be dropped out of sight, it is critically important that the financial support accorded to *bona fides* astronomy should be at least equivalent to that given to the astronomical segments of NASA.

CHAPTER TWO

Know Then Thyself

"Know then thyself" was a precept of the ancient Greeks. It appears also in a well-known poem of Pope. The first two lines read, "Know then thyself, presume not God to scan, the proper study of mankind is man." The second line has become almost a cliché. Nowadays scientists take Pope's two injunctions quite seriously. We do not presume God to scan, if by God you mean an inquiry into the purpose of the Universe. The problems which such an inquiry would set would be too difficult. We are content to seek in a groping fashion for the laws that govern the Universe. The problem of why these laws and not others is so far completely beyond us. It might surprise you that I am referring to God in this fashion, as if God were a set of laws, a logical structure. But what else would you have? The older ideas of God, what I might call the classical ideas, on which formal religions are based, are all too obviously simple social concepts derived from everyday experience. The notion of God the Father is obviously taken from the father as head of his family. Other aspects of God which appear throughout the Bible are equally plainly taken from the concept of the leader as head of his people. Throughout the Old Testament, God is even cast in the role of a successful war leader, the kind of man that is so frequently elevated to the head of state.

Of course these are not the only concepts of religion to be found in the Old Testament of the Bible. God is quite naturally all wise, but this is far less important than the concept of God as a lawmaker and of God's anger at those who break His laws. It is this concept of law that has given the religion of the Hebrews its special quality. The notions of God the Father, God the successful war leader, are present in almost all religions. They are simple notions, almost childish. But the notion of God as a lawmaker, not subject to irrational fits or changes of point of view, such as we find in the Greek gods, was something new and important. To be sure, the laws in which God was supposed to be interested were obvious extrapolations of ordinary social laws, the kind of law we find it necessary to have in a civilized community. They were a first attempt to build a logical structure which was the essence of God. It was this feature of the religion of the Hebrews that gave it a special importance over the religions of other peoples.

When I said at the outset that by God I meant the system of laws that govern the Universe, what are often called the laws of physics, I was making a direct extrapolation from the basic concept of the Hebrews. I was replacing the simple earthly concept of law—that you must not drive your car through a red light—by the most subtle logical structure of which I can conceive. These are the physical laws, which so far we struggle to find and not to question.

And so if we do not presume God to scan, then what of man? A great deal of progress has been made since Pope's day in understanding the nature of man. We now look back in something like astonishment on what was perhaps the most important step, not because it represented something incredibly subtle or profound, but because it was so obvious. It is astonishing because it was found so difficult, and yet it could hardly have been easier. I am referring to the discovery of the nineteenth century, the discovery of Darwin and Wallace, that man is an animal. One would think the most casual glance at the world would suffice to convince everybody of this. You do not need to be an anatomical expert to perceive that the skeletal structure of a man is strikingly similar to that of an ape. Yet it was necessary for the nineteenth century to go into incredible detail in order to convince itself that this was so. To the twentieth-century mind, Darwin's book *The Origin of Species* is a fantastic exercise in the obvious. Yet without it the nineteenth century would not have believed the obvious. Plainly other factors besides the issue of man as an animal entered the argument. Human beings are not so stupid that they cannot perceive the obvious when they have no strong incentive to believe otherwise. Plainly the strong incentive in this case was the Bible. Acceptance of man as an animal implied that one must not go on believing implicitly in everything that was said in the Bible, for the Bible asserted that man had been placed by God above the animals. It was because of this that it was necessary to drive the case home with relentless logic; and the outcome has been that very many of us no longer do believe implicitly in the Bible.

The issue was not merely a scientific one. It implied a profound social readjustment throughout Western civilization. What I said at the outset concerning the meaning of God could not have been said at all in the early nineteenth century. I am not referring here to the danger of religious persecution, but to the fact that the human mind was inhibited against such thoughts. The brain had been so conditioned in childhood that it was incapable of entertaining certain thoughts, in this case the fallibility of the Bible. I mention all of this not by way of attacking religion but to raise what seems to me an important question. How far are we inhibited against certain obvious thought patterns today? How far does our childhood training prevent us from seeing the obvious? Was the nineteenth century the very last period in human history when people suffered from such blind prejudices that the obvious could not be seen? Clearly not, I would say; an affirmative answer would surely be a manifest case of special pleading. Hence I conclude that there must be some perfectly straightforward big truths around us which we are all too stupid to see. The dilemma is that the search for them is immediately blocked by one's own prejudices. We are prisoners of our own mold of thought, of the mold of thought of our present society, and it is excessively difficult to break loose from the strait jacket in which we are clamped.

It is not sufficient merely to want to break loose from our prison. It is not too difficult to discipline oneself to think more or less without inhibitions along any new line of thought that may present itself. In a large measure the physicists of the twentieth century have learned to do this. But they have also learned that in addition to being willing to explore new lines of thought without prejudice it is also necessary to get the right lines of thought. How are these to be decided? Lack of prejudice in attempting to solve a problem is not sufficient to guarantee that an unusual avenue of attack will open itself to you, still less the correct avenue of attack. The difficulty is that we find ourselves in intellectual blinkers that simply prevent us from looking the right way. It is almost a matter of principle that in any difficult unsolved problem the right method of attack has not been found; failure to solve important problems is rarely due to inadequacy in the handling of technical details. Yet knowing that you have not got the right line of attack does not help very much. It is also necessary that some new and quite unexpected concept should arise in your mind. And this will not happen just by demanding that it shall come about.

I think what it comes down to is that one must depend

on chance. The brain gets lots of opportunities to think outside its usual patterns, but only in brief flashes. These brief flashes occur, it seems to me, after our thought patterns have been dissolved for some reason, and at the precise moment when they reform. There can be a moment every morning when you wake from sleep when the things you were working on yesterday reform themselves. Better still, when you are on vacation, and your work is temporarily forgotten, odd and unusual aspects of it may suddenly present themselves. This is the sort of way in which new ideas are born. And sometimes an idea may occur to you due to a remark from someone else, provided the remark throws your thoughts into momentary confusion. These are the brief fleeting occasions on which you might hit something entirely new.

Although I am a little off the main track of my argument now, I think this whole question of originality, whether in relation to science or in relation to social problems, is worth pursuing a little further. For the reasons I have just given everybody has access to new ideas. It seems to me that originality cannot be the perquisite of the few. In everybody, the brain must occasionally flash away for a brief moment along some unusual track. But this is not to say that such brief flashes will be anything more than mere nonsense, of no more use than the flashes we call dreams. Indeed these flashes clearly take the place, so far as our thought processes are concerned, of the biologists' mutations. And we know that the overwhelming proportion of biological mutations are harmful. In a similar way the overwhelming proportion of new ideas are rubbish. The proportion of rubbish can be cut down, however, by the possession of a sound technique. I believe that a thorough understanding of what has already been achieved in any subject is necessary to originality. You cannot come to a subject like physics without possessing a sound knowledge of physics and mathematics, as well as a detailed knowledge of the particular problem in question, and expect to have a good idea. The brain must already possess appropriate building blocks out of which a new idea and its application can be fashioned. This of course is why hard years of technical study about the subject, in general, and hard weeks of preparation in the problem, in particular, must precede moments of originality. Yet even this is not sufficient.

In its nature a new idea lives for only a brief moment unless it is nurtured. Even after it has been brought into the light of explicit consciousness a new idea is very easily killed. And I am referring now not merely to bad ideas but to good ones, even to ideas that turn out to be of critical importance. There are many known cases in physics where men have had ideas which subsequently turn out to be correct and which they have killed in their own brains. The curious paradox is that it tends to be the technically most competent men that are the greatest murderers of new ideas. Their technical faculties are so well developed that they see the snags and difficulties in any new idea far too soon. Every proposal is instantly subjected to a blast of analysis that inevitably destroys it. This of course is a clear gain in the vast majority of cases, because in the vast majority of cases new ideas are wrong, but unfortunately it also eliminates the small fraction of worthwhile new steps. In a very real sense, originality becomes harder the cleverer you are.

I think it should be possible for anyone, however clever, to discipline himself in this matter. There seem to be one or two simple rules that it should be possible to observe. First, never bring your critical faculties to bear too soon on a new idea. Use your technique to encourage it. Then as it gains strength expose a new idea more and more to criticism. If after early encouragement an idea cannot stand up to later criticism then throw it out by all means. But give everything a chance to root itself. However, the later subjection of ideas to a thorough critical assessment is just as important as early tolerance. It is here that your crank fails. Your crank is thoroughly tolerant of every idea he has and so escapes the fault of the razor-sharp analyst. But he fails, and his ideas are useless, because he has no worthwhile rejection mechanism. The piercing analyst and the crank are at opposite extremes of a spectrum, and the problem is to fit oneself into the right place between them.

It was notions such as these that I had in mind when I said at the University of Washington last Spring that the whole of human society could become upset, or even disintegrated, by two or three sheets of paper, if the right words were written on them. If an appropriate series of flashes, of new ideas, ideas related to our state of society, were set out so that we could all be infected by them, enormous changes and enormous social forces would be released. It is perhaps fortunate, as I said then, that none of us is in a position to deliver to the newspapers tomorrow morning such sheets of paper. It is not only difficult to come by our flashes of new perception but no two of us have flashes exactly in the same direction. Even if you should suddenly see a point in some particular problem or other, even if you should be right, you have still got the job of convincing the rest of us. And this will turn out to hold you up for quite a long time! In the remainder of this chapter I am going to describe some of my own particular flashes concerning the subject that I set myself at the beginning, the nature of man. I might as well confess at the outset that before the end I will lose myself, but you would hardly expect that it could be otherwise.

Let me take up the argument with evolution, the evolution that has led from the first living organisms to man. Looking back along this chain, this incredibly detailed chain of many steps, I am overwhelmingly impressed by the way in which chemistry has gradually given way to electronics. It is not unreasonable to describe the first living creatures as entirely chemical in character. Although electrochemical processes are important in plants, organized electronics, in the sense of data processing, does not enter or operate in the plant world. But primitive electronics begins to assume importance as soon as we have a creature that moves around, instead of being rooted in a particular spot, as a plant is. This is surely what we mean by an animal, a creature that moves around. In order to move in any purposeful way a system capable of analyzing and processing information about the external world, about the lay of the land as one might say, becomes necessary. The first electronic systems possessed by primitive animals were essentially guidance systems, analogous logically to sonar or radar. As we pass to more developed animals we find electronic systems being used not merely for guidance but for directing the animal toward food, particularly toward food in the form of another animal. First we have animals eating plants, then animals eating animals, a second order effect. The situation is analogous to a guided missile, the job of which is to intercept and destroy another missile. Just as in our modern world attack and defense become more and more subtle in their methods, so it was the case with animals. And with increasing subtlety, better and better systems of electronics become necessary. What happened in nature has a close parallel with the development of electronics in modern military applications.

I find it a sobering thought that but for the tooth-and-claw existence of the jungle we should not possess our intellectual capabilities, we should not be able to inquire into the structure of the Universe, or to be able to appreciate a symphony of Beethoven. What happened was that electronic systems gradually outran their original purposes. At first they existed to guide animals with powerful weapons, teeth and claws, toward their victims. The astonishing thing, however, was that at a certain stage of subtlety the teeth and claws became unnecessary. Creatures began to emerge in which the original roles of chemistry and electronics were reversed. Instead of the electronics being servant to the chemistry, the reverse became the case. By the time we reach the human, the body has become the servant of the head, existing very largely to supply the brain with appropriate materials for its operation. In us, the computer in our heads, the computer that we call our brain, has entirely taken control. The same I think is true of most of the higher animals, indeed I think this is how one really defines a higher animal. Viewed in this light, the question that is sometimes asked—can computers think?—is somewhat ironic. Here of course I mean the computers that we ourselves make out of inorganic materials. What on earth do those who ask such a question think they themselves are? Simply computers, but vastly more complicated ones than anything we have yet learned to make. Remember that our man-made computer industry is a mere two or three decades old, whereas we ourselves are the products of an evolution that has operated over hundreds of millions of years.

Before I leave this subject of evolution I would like to say something about its beginning and something about its end, about its beginnings perhaps a thousand million years ago and about what has happened during the last 50,000 years or so. How did the beginning of life occur?

I was involved in an argument with a chemist about this problem a while ago. He was very impressed by the length of time it took to get life started here on the Earth. We know that the Earth was formed some 4.5 billion years ago, whereas the development of life has probably been confined to the latter half of this great time span. Why did it take 2 billion years or more to get started? My chemist friend thought that it might mean that the formation of life was a very slow process, and of course in a literal sense this must be true. But you can think of the problem in two quite different ways. Suppose the origin of life requires a very large number of small steps, for example, 50,000 such steps, and suppose that the time span required for each step is in the region of 100,000 years, there is something like a 50 percent chance of the next step happening. Then some steps will take more than 100,000 years and some less, but in total the whole thing will add up to a billion years or so. This in essence was my chemist's point of view. But the picture could really be very much different, and this was the case I was urging. It is certainly true that many small steps were required in the beginning of life, but the situation could equally be that most of the small steps happened quite quickly and easily. The bottleneck could have been a small number of major events. They could have depended upon a few key developments in the history of the Earth, of a physical and geographical nature. The difference between these two points of view comes when you consider whether the origin of life here on the Earth was inevitable. On the first view all you have to do is to wait sufficiently long. On the second view everything turns on a small number of major improbabilities. For some planets the major improbabilities would occur, on others they would not, whereas according to the first view life would inevitably arise on all planets given sufficient time. My opinion is that we have to deal with the second case. The same thing was true, I think, about later biological evolution. I suspect there has been a number of major turning points in evolution, perhaps only a quite small number. Consider the evolution of the mammals. This may well have turned on the development of a particular plant, grass. Before grass developed, comparatively recently in the evolutionary time scale, mammals may have been impossible. But once grass was here, mammals—and ultimately ourselves—were probably inevitable.

Clearly when we come to the last 50,000 years or so a similar turning point has been passed. This came I think with the development of communication, with the ability of our brains to pass information from one to the other by means of speech. Notice the sequence of remarkable steps. First you have electronics for simple guidance, then for attack and defense, then electronics take over the whole control, and finally one electronic system succeeds in making contact with other similar systems. With this final step the race between attack and defense was virtually over. No other animal could then compete, the situation being essentially as decisive as it must have been when the first self-replicating creature outstripped its nonreplicating chemical competitors. I do not think that humans are necessarily much cleverer than other animals, taken as lone individuals. I do not think that the cleverest among us would appear too bright if all we had received from our parents and acquaintances were grunts, squeaks, and cuffs on the ear. I doubt whether in such circumstances even the greatest human mathematician would have reached the standard of intellect of the average child of 10. The remarkable thing nowadays is that not only each of us carries the whole evolution of our species in the physical sense in our bodies, but we also carry, at any rate partially, the cultural evolution. None of us is remotely like what we would have been but for the ideas we have received from others. Whenever you hear a remark that sets you thinking upon a new trend you are not quite the same person you were before. It is, I would say, this special power, related very closely to what we call education, that constitutes the special ability of the human species.

All this can be put in computer terminology. Our brains are specially set up to receive input data from the external world. Through the eyes we receive information about the physical nature of the world around us. With our ears we receive information about the presence of other creatures, and so forth. The same is true for other animals, but what other animals have not succeeded in doing is to use the natural vehicles of input to the brain, the eye and the ear, as a means of passing great quantities of data from one to another of them. The special power of the human has been to adapt the natural vehicles of input to the brain, natural in the sense that they were originally used and developed to acquire information about the external world, to the quite different purpose I have just mentioned. Of course the critical step, the amazingly clever step, was to be able to convert one's thoughts—the operations of one's consciousness if you like—into a coded system of sounds by means of the lips. From a computer point of view it is not difficult to see that, clever as it may be, this system is rather makeshift. A much more direct electronic output and input from one brain to another would be preferable, but so far this has not been achieved, and we must make do with what we have got. Quite plainly a large fraction of the misunderstandings and quarrels that occur among human beings are due to the inadequacies of our methods of communication. The point I am making is that to have any system of communication is enormously better than none.

Once human beings had become in a considerable degree independent of other animals, once we were no longer threatened by other animals, human social evolution proceeded in a way that was strikingly analogous to that of long-term biological evolution. We find different human communities vying with each other in much the way that different species of animals competed with each other in the old days. In the rivalries and wars of different states we have something closely analogous to the old tooth-and-claw existence. Indeed we have here a large fraction of the social problems that still face us today, and about which I shall be speaking in later chapters. As I have already pointed out, this rivalry has even led us into mocking the gradual biological development from chemical to electronic evolution. The road from the bow and arrow or the spear to the IBM computer is not much different in its logic from the long road that separates man from the earliest animals.

"Know then thyself." I hope that what I have said represents some small progress along the track we must follow to knowing ourselves. What are we? The simple answer coming out of my remarks is that each of us is a complex electronic computer. You may feel there is something unsatisfactory in this, and I tend to agree. My objections are not the conventional ones, however. I do not object on any grounds of principle to being a computer. If I am a computer, well too bad maybe, but then I am a computer. My difficulties arise over the experience of consciousness. I am not raising the old chestnut of how can a computer think. The issue it seems to me is much more subtle than that. I am not even too much worried by consciousness taken as a whole. For by consciousness one can obviously mean the operations that exist in a certain defined part of a computer. In manmade computers we already think in terms of active and non-active parts of the internal store. One could think for instance of the arithmetic processing units of an ordinary computer as the consciousness of the computer, and one could think of its backing storage, its magnetic tapes, as the subconscious. My difficulty with consciousness is that it forces on one a concept that lies outside physics, the concept of the present, the present moment of time. According to physics the events that constitute the physical world form a four-dimensional continuum, and physics does not permit us to attach any more significance to one moment of time than to another. There is no such thing as the present moment in the motion of the Earth around the Sun. What the theory of gravitation tells us is the complete motion of the Earth around the Sun, comprising its past motion, its present position, and its future; we get the whole story all at once. When we break it up into a past, present, and future, we do so subjectively.

This sharp difference between physical theory and subjective experience has led some physicists to suggest that subjective experience is illusory, that there is no such thing as the present. But there is a clear-cut contradiction in such an argument, for in all our experiments and observations the concept of the present and of subjective consciousness is widely used. We make no bones about trusting our subjective present when we carry out an observation, or when we analyze the results of an experiment. We stand then on no subtleties, we take our subjective present at its face value. So I think either we must make a serious attempt to analyze logically the subjective present, demanded so clearly by our consciousness, or we must have grave doubts about the whole experimental evidence for our physical theories. Since in the latter case we would essentially have no physics at all, I prefer to attempt a discussion of the meaning of the subjective present.

Subjectively we have this uncanny feeling that the world evolves from moment to moment, and indeed the whole of my previous discussion of biological evolution was predicated on this concept. You might, if you are a physicist, object to what I am trying to develop now, but did you object to what I said before? I doubt whether life could proceed at all in a normal fashion if we did not have this concept of an evolution in time. You could have no idea of where you would be going when you left this hall, because the concept would be meaningless. There could be no such thing as airline schedules or indeed any planning for the future or any discussion of the past. It would be essential to take life as a complete whole, as if one were to play a symphony by striking every note in the complete score all at once.

The problem it seems to me can be formulated as follows. Take the whole of a person's life. The events that describe the subjective present form a subclass out of the sum totality of all of the events that constitute either your life or mine. How is that subclass to be defined? Here I want a definition that is not pure mysticism, but which corresponds in a proper way to the logical standards that are current in mathematics and physics. I said at an earlier stage in this chapter that I would end at a point of confusion and now I have done so. For I can offer no

serious answer to this question. What is apparently
needed is a series of markers, just as in a book we divide
up what is being said into a series of sentences by means
of periods. The difficulty is that, to make much sense,
the markers should be places where the usual sequence
of cause and effect is interrupted. So long as the sequence of cause and effect is continuous there seems to
be no possibility of dividing up the full totality of our
experience. This is the dilemma for the case of the Earth
moving around the Sun, for instance.

The solution to the problem, and I feel that a solution
there must be, may lie at one or another of two sensitive
points of physics. It is well known that in modern quantum theory uncertainty exists, that in apparently identical circumstances a physical system will sometimes do
one thing and sometimes another. At one time it was believed that the uncertainty arose from the observer's in-
terference with whatever physical system he happened
to be looking at. Nowadays I do not think the notion of
the observer himself introducing the uncertainty is very
widely believed. Indeed Schrödinger, many years ago,
expressed the situation very well. You put a cat in a box,
point a loaded gun at its head, and arrange that the gun is
either fired or not by means of some quantum criterion.
For example, you arrange that the physical mechanism
which pulls the trigger is activated for one half-life of
some radioactive substance. If decay occurs the gun is
fired, if not the trigger mechanism is switched off. You
then close the lid of the box and go away for a couple of

days' vacation. When you return you open up the box and the question is: Does your raising the lid of the box really decide whether you find the cat to be shot or not? I suspect that most physicists of the younger generation today believe that opening the lid of the box has nothing at all to do with what is found inside, and I think this was Schrödinger's point. What it comes down to is that our calculations contain uncertainty about what is going to happen, but I do not think that the Universe—more precisely a physical system—behaves with any uncertainty, it makes one definite decision or the other. If one takes this point of view it is necessary to say that while the Universe is entirely decisive, our powers of calculations are not, and if we believe a famous investigation due to von Neumann, our calculations never can be decisive. This is one of the two sensitive points.

In spite of a recent fragment of experimental evidence to the contrary, there is strong reason to believe that the laws of physics are time symmetric. That is to say it is equally possible for a series of events, any series of events you like, to take place in a sequence from future to past as it is in the more normal sequence from past to future. The thermodynamicist naturally objects to this, stating firmly that certain sequences are never observed, for example, a kettle of boiling water placed on a gas stove has never been observed to become a kettle containing cold water. Yet the time symmetry of the physical laws would permit this to happen. If one considers all the possible initial states of a physical system and all the possible final states, the two sets are identical. For every initial state *a* changing into a final state *b* there is an initial state *b* that changes into *a*. The problem of thermodynamics is to explain why certain initial states are excluded in the actual world. So long as we limit initial states to a subclass of all the possible initial states, then thermodynamics, in particular the second law of thermodynamics, can be operative. But if all initial states were permitted the second law would be nonsense. Now what decides the restriction of the initial states to a particular subclass? Manifestly the external conditions. In the last analysis this becomes a cosmological problem involving the whole Universe. So it would seem clear that the phenomenon of the sense of time, if not the phenomenon of the subjective present, resides in the Universe at large. And it may well be the case that the same is true of the first sensitive point, the uncertainty that exists in quantum theory. It could be that our methods of calculation for an isolated system become uncertain simply because we have separated our system from the rest of the Universe, we have cut its connections as it were, and that without knowing what those connections happen to be, uncertainty is inevitable.

In some way such as this, by an interaction with the external world, it may be that the problem of the subjective consciousness can be solved. It seems in some degree significant that in attempting to analyze ourselves it is our normal practice to think of ourselves as discrete units, closed boxes, embedded in bone and skin. It should not be surprising that this point of view fails at some point, just as I am sure it does in the discussion of other isolated systems in the physical world. And it may well be that without understanding in a more subtle way the connections between ourselves and the external world no complete knowledge of ourselves is possible. I would like to end by giving you in full the quotation from Pope.

> Know then thyself, presume not God to scan;
> The proper study of mankind is man.
> Placed on this isthmus of a middle state,
> A being darkly wise, and rudely great:
> With too much knowledge for the sceptic side,
> With too much weakness for the stoic's pride,
> He hangs between; in doubt to act or rest;
> In doubt to deem himself a god, or beast;
> In doubt his mind or body to prefer;
> Born but to die, and reasoning but to err;
> Alike in ignorance, his reason such,
> Whether he thinks too little or too much;
> Chaos of thought and passion, all confused;
> Still by himself abused, or disabused;
> Created half to rise, and half to fall;
> Great lord of all things, yet a prey to all;
> Sole judge of truth, in endless error hurled;
> The glory, jest, and riddle of the world!

CHAPTER THREE

Further Reflections on
the Subjective Present

Since writing the previous chapter, a disturbing fantasy has occurred to me. It is possible to get rid of the subjective present, provided we suppose the existence of a *choice machine*.

I do not think our subjective consciousness is in serious opposition to the postulate that consciousness is made up of a sequence of discrete events—or a sequence of packets of events. It is true that we have the over-all impression of a smooth flow of consciousness, but we certainly experience plenty of sudden jerks from one state to another. So there seems little objection to assuming that even the smooth flow can be broken up into small enough discrete packets, rather as an apparently continuous film can broken up into discrete frames. Let the sequence be denoted by ψ_1, ψ_2, . . . , ψ_n. Let all these states belong to the physical world and let there be a sequential order $1, 2, . . . , n$, corresponding to the usual subjective relationships of cause and effect.

Now let the choice machine single out any one of these states, ψ_r say. The action of the choice machine causes us to experience the consciousness of state r. Next let the machine single out ψ_s, *where* the state s has *no particular relation* to the state r. Proceed in this way, letting the machine choose states *at random*. This procedure produces the effect of time "as an ever-rolling stream," *even though the choices may occur in any order whatsoever*. At state ψ_r one would have the subjective impression of having "just lived through" the immediately preceding states ψ_{r-1}, ψ_{r-2}, ... The choice machine could flash about, jumping from childhood to old age to middle age to old age to youth, and we should never know it. The cause-and-effect relations in the sequence $1, 2, \ldots, n$ would dominate our consciousness. In this way, the subjective present can be entirely replaced by a procedure of choice. Indeed, one could go through every one of the states an infinite number of times and never know it.

The important question is whether anything is gained by substituting a choice machine for the subjective present. My impression is that a great deal may be gained, because I suspect that such a machine must be introduced into physics, if the quantum theory is to have logical consistency. Here I must admit that I do not understand the usual expositions of quantum theory, and I will try to explain why.

Let ψ_1, ψ_2, . . . , be the states representing some microscopic system, and let Ψ_1, Ψ_2, . . . , be states representing a macroscopic apparatus. The ordering of the states are to be such that, when the microscopic system is coupled with the macroscopic system in a certain way, ψ_r goes with Ψ_r for all r. That is to say, the wave function for the whole coupled system is

$$\Sigma_r \, a_r \, \psi_r \, \Psi_r,$$

in which the a_r are certain (time-dependent) coefficients. Now take a look at the macroscopic system. Because the macroscopic system is classical it is possible to determine with certainty which of the states Ψ_1, . . . , the macroscopic system is "in." Hence, after the coupling, it is possible to determine which of the states ψ_1, . . . , the microscopic system is "in."

If I am right in supposing this to be the usual argument, whereby the wave function for a microscopic state is "condensed" into a particular eigen-state of some specified operator, I find myself in revolt against the basis of quantum theory. The sentence beginning: "Because the macroscopic system is classical . . ." appears to me to be nonsense. Macroscopic systems are not classical, they are quantum systems containing more particles than a microscopic system, nothing else. It is just as invalid to choose a particular wave function $\psi_r \, \Psi_r$ from the mixed wave function $\Sigma_r \, a_r \, \psi_r \, \Psi_r$ as it would have been to choose ψ_r from a mixed wave function $\Sigma_r \, b_r \, \psi_r$.

Every student of quantum theory is cautioned against the following procedure for dealing with $\Sigma_r \, b_r \, \psi_r$. Take each ψ_r and calculate forward in time for any specified interval, using the machinery of quantum theory, then combine the results for each state according to the probability $|b_r|^2$. This procedure is known to give a bad approximation, interference effects between different states being lost. Yet we are not only encouraged to do something rather like this, when we couple to a classical apparatus, but we are instructed to interpret the probability moduli in a curious way. If we choose ψ_r Ψ_r, on the basis of what our "classical apparatus" tells us, we do so with unit probability, not with probability $|a_r|^2$. However, we argue that the probability of the classical apparatus telling us to do this is $|a_r|^2$, and under suitable circumstances we find that $|a_r|^2$ for the coupled system is proportional to $|b_r|^2$ for the microscopic system.

When one looks a little further, a classical apparatus is always a chunk of equipment with a human observer tacked on to it. We calculate that in a certain time interval there is a 50-percent probability of one of a number of radioactive nuclei undergoing decay. We couple our classical apparatus—a counter or a bubble chamber—to the decay, in such a way that a very definite event is correlated with decay (essentially with unit probability) and another definite event is correlated with nondecay (also essentially with unit probability). For example, the appearance or the nonappearance of a trail in the chamber constitutes such definite events. So far no human is involved—except in the sense that humans have put the equipment together. Having done so they can simply lock up the laboratory, like closing the lid of the box in Schrödinger's cat example.

Now my impression is that not until we ourselves

"take a look" do we ever adopt the steps described
above. Only when we take a look do we "condense" the
wave function. Any attempt at condensation without
taking a look will lead to a loss of information, to a
poorer description of the behavior of the physical system
in question. After taking a look, on the other hand, *we
seem to improve the information content of the system.*
We give a definite answer as to whether an ionization
trail has appeared in the bubble chamber, or to whether
Schrödinger's cat is still alive. It is as if we ourselves,
through our consciousness, *can act as choice machines.*
Hence I conclude that choice machines exist. I am one
myself. But this is not to say that I myself am the primary choice machine. What could be taking place is that
I am aware, through my consciousness, of connections
with the external world and that the choice machine
affects not just me but the whole Universe.

Go back now to the states of consciousness which I
wrote above as a single sequence ψ_1, ψ_2, ψ_3, ... There
could be multiple sequences, with several alternatives for
each ψ_r, depending on quantum considerations. For example we could have

$$\psi_1 \nearrow \psi_2', \psi_3', \ldots ,$$
$$\searrow \psi_2'', \psi_3'', \ldots ,$$

with a forking point at ψ_2 depending on, say, the decay
or the nondecay of a nucleus. The sequences ψ_1, ψ_2', ψ_3',
. . . , and ψ_1, ψ_2'', ψ_3'', . . . , could then proceed quite

differently. The total number of sequences that could be accumulated in a "lifetime" would then be enormous. So long as the sequences remain rigidly separated, with ψ_2' unrelated to (unaware of) ψ_2'', the choice machine could hop about indiscriminately among the sequences, without our having the subjective impression of living more than one life. We could "live" millions of decisively different lives in this way, and never know it. One cannot be subjectively aware of being killed by a quantum criterion, because one cannot be subjectively aware of the termination of a sequence. Schrödinger's cat has only the one continuing sequence, that in which it is not shot. The rest of us, however, have two sequences, one with the cat shot, the other with it alive.

CHAPTER FOUR

Education and Research

Nowadays, children and teen-agers get a pretty soft time of it. Nothing must be done to offend their tender susceptibilities. They are allowed to loll for long hours in front of television sets, they refuse to walk anywhere if transportation is available, and if transportation is not available, they probably will not walk anyway. This lazy, good-for-nothing treatment of children used to be thought, by the Western world in general, to be the doubtful privilege of the United States. I remember not long ago the way Britishers and Europeans laughed at the upbringing of children in the United States. The irony is that they now do almost exactly the same themselves. The situation seems to be that the rearing of children is very much a function of the state of society, particularly of its technological state. The more primitive the technology is, the harder kids are expected to work. In a society at subsistence level, young children of 2 or 3 go out into the fields to work alongside their parents. In our so-called advanced societies very little is required up to the age of 20, and should an individual child feel impelled to hard work in any direction, except that of sports, it will find a thousand and one stumbling blocks placed in its path. It will soon become disheartened, frustrated, and, worst of all, bored.

The picture changes sharply when a young person reaches the twenties. The student in graduate school suddenly finds the standards that he or she is expected to reach have become raised far above anything they had previously conceived possible. The situation may well be worse for the young person who goes out into the business world, into our modern equivalent of the tooth-and-claw struggles of the jungle. From the age of 20 to about 35 our modern society demands its pound of flesh. There are no more long hours of lolling in front of the television set. The young person is not thrown immediately, and unceremoniously, into a prison cell. Instead, the prison is slowly erected around him. As Wordsworth put it: "Shades of the prison-house begin to close upon the growing boy." It happened sooner in Wordsworth's time, nowadays the critical years are from 25 to 35. A few succeed. At a comparatively young age they become prosperous, they ease out into a relaxed life that bears some resemblance to their childhood. For this to happen, a man needs great energy, ability, and perhaps not a little luck. In the maze that constitutes our modern world, an occasional pathway can be found leading away from the crowded freeways of commerce, which carries the lucky traveler into pleasant country. But in such cases others soon follow behind, and the quiet pathway itself becomes a thoroughfare.

There are many who do not manage to escape the clutches of society, but who can nevertheless be described as highly successful. These are the corporation men. I think it was *Time* magazine that first invented the journalistic trick of preceding a man's name by the organization to which he belonged—John Smith, instead of being known as John Smith, became Du Pont's Smith, if he happened to work for the Du Pont Corporation, or Rhode Island's Smith, if he happened to be a politician from Rhode Island. In this way the individual was made subservient to the organization to which he belonged. This journalistic trick has caught on, and is now used all over the world, showing clearly that today we live in the age of organization not in the age of the individual. The pitiful thing is that to begin with poor John Smith feels quite flattered by having a powerful organization, with all its prestige, immediately preceding his own name. A good deal probably depends on John Smith's age. If he is young, he will feel that the prestige of the organization is helpful to his career. But as he grows older, as he reaches the peak of his career, he will realize how much of his achievements he owes to his organization, how little to himself. He will come at last to see that his career would collapse in ruins should he detach himself from his particular organization. He sees indeed that the organization owns him, just as *Time* magazine's journalistic phrase implies.

The less successful by the age of 35, and by the term *successful* I am using a mere monetary standard, realize that the struggle is not worth the candle. They pack it in and accept what they have got, and so avoid the ulcers of the more successful. Their existence would indeed be more pleasant than one might expect if it were not for the tricks and devices which the more successful have thought up in order to relieve them of what little money they have got. I am referring now to the incessant barrage of advertising gimmicks to which we are constantly subjected. It is true that we all develop almost complete impermeability to the advertising media, and it is utterly necessary that we should do so. Anyone taking literally the advice of the salesmen, who are always telling us that such and such a product is exactly what we need, would be drunk the whole time, would find themselves smoking so much that they would develop lung cancer within a week. But although our insulation may be almost complete, for none of us is remotely stupid enough to swallow the stuff dished up to us by the advertising media, the whole thing is a preposterous irritation. And the less you are able to beat society in the financial sense the more you are exposed to it.

I have been using the word *successful* in a loose way. By successful I simply mean someone who has an income above, perhaps substantially above, the average. It is an inevitable logical consequence of this definition that not everybody can be successful. Lack of success, in this sense, is the necessary burden of the majority. And in a society that emphasizes the importance of success it is inevitable that the majority of people will find themselves asking the following question: What might I have done that would have made a difference to my life? What did I leave undone that I ought to have done?

There are quite a few things that prove a great help in life. To have a father or a relative or a friend who can give you the right business opportunity at the right moment is an obvious case in point. But such things are a matter of luck. No reasonable person could seriously lay blame on such factors as this. In reviewing a misspent life you clearly think about what might have been possible, not what you would have done if you had been born with a golden spoon in your mouth. You look for some genuinely important factor that was indeed within your grasp. Many people find such a factor, the factor we refer to as education. There is undeniable evidence that completely apart from intellectual ability a man who attends college has a better chance than one who does not. Nowadays a college education is regarded as a necessity for many jobs that were done quite satisfactorily a generation ago by people who had not gone within ten miles of any college. Once again what started as an American trend is also becoming common practice in Europe.

The snobbery exists, the barriers exist, and it is natural therefore that those who have been excluded in any one generation should feel that they do not wish their children to be excluded in a like fashion. Hence the present emphasis on education. Hence the incredible growth in

the last years of universities, private and state-supported
alike, throughout the United States. And the same thing
is following behind in Europe, only a few years behind.
In Britain we have started a crop of new universities, and
the older ones are being rapidly expanded. Noteworthy
as this may seem it may still only be quite small compared to what is to come in the future. Not long ago I
heard a discussion between two university presidents in
which it was said that the money spent on education by
the federal government might eventually rival that spent
on defense. At first, I took this to be something of an ex-
aggeration, but on further thought I saw there were
deeper ramifications than I had imagined.

We know today that Karl Marx in reaching his con-
clusion that capitalist societies would eventually collapse
inward on themselves overlooked a very simple point.
And indeed Western economists also overlooked it for
an almost incredibly long time: that the economy can be
stabilized through the government controlling about 20
percent of the gross national product. The control acts
like the building of a reservoir. A reservoir prevents
floods, and it helps to eliminate droughts. In a similar
fashion government control of perhaps 20 percent of the
national product largely eliminates the gross fluctuations
of boom and slump that occurred in the first 30 years of
the century. Now this control raises a problem. Expressed in terms of money, what is a government going
to spend its 20 percent on? In principle, the control could
be operated simply by digging large holes in the ground

and then filling them in again, as the economist Keynes pointed out. But so far no one has been willing to pursue this extreme of economic logic. Governments naturally look for projects on which they can spend their money in a responsible fashion. So far, defense has consumed some 50 percent of government spending. But a very real issue arises as to whether this will be possible in the future. We have now reached the stage where the United States could probably kill every inhabitant of the Earth ten times over, or at any rate this stage will eventually be reached. Where one wonders does one go from there? Of course one must always try for a defense against the other fellow, but both logic and expert opinion suggest that defense against nuclear weapons is not a serious possibility. The picture genuinely seems to emerge that, in the future, defense spending, if it continues on the present scale, will indeed become the equivalent of digging holes in the ground. In the long term it is likely that defense spending will gradually be cut back. What, one wonders, will take its place? Education is certainly one possibility. I shall raise another possibility in the next chapter.

By now I have laid out the ground plan of my present argument. Education is already a big affair, it may get bigger, it has popular support behind it. I want to examine what factors in the situation seem to me favorable and what seem unfavorable. So far I have been concerned with social arguments for education. There is also an intellectual argument.

In the previous chapter I drew your attention to the remarkable ability of the human species, the ability that separates us from other animals, to combine together the knowledge, experience, and discoveries of a large number of people and to write the whole totality on a single human brain. None of us is really an individual, we each carry with us the whole intellectual and social development of our species. The process by which this happens is education, whether formal education in our schools and universities or informal education in the home. It is not unreasonable to say that it is education that separates us from the other animals. Hence there can be no argument about the importance of education; and I do not think there can be much complaint if education should eventually take over the running from the defense program in our economy.

It is a strange thought that if by some means the process of education could be interrupted for a period no longer than the life span of the individual human our whole species would revert to Stone-Age conditions. It is supposed by some that such an eventuality might actually happen in the event of a nuclear war. For myself I do not believe that this is so. I think that once living creatures follow the track that we humans have followed in the last ten or twenty thousand years the process is quite irreversible. Nothing can stop it short of complete extermination of the species. I like to think of these problems in terms of rather fantastic examples. Suppose that some new virus appeared which had an equivalent effect on the human species that myxamotosis had on rabbits. Suppose also that very young children were most resistant to the new virus, as would be entirely reasonable. Suppose that everybody over the age of 5 died. What would happen? The situation would obviously be chaotic by any standards that we can imagine, even by the standards of a nuclear war. But I have no doubt that some children would survive and grow to adult life. Would they revert to the Stone Age? On the whole I doubt it. I think there would be some with the intellectual curiosity to puzzle out what all the things around them meant. Some would learn to read, and slowly but surely the old knowledge would be recovered.

You will realize therefore that when I say there are many aspects of education about which I am unhappy my objections do not apply to education in principle. I have referred already to the social aspects of education. I object very strongly to the whole idea of a college education as a meal ticket. I suspect the fact that education is becoming a sacred cow in our society is not at all connected with its intrinsic value but with this meal-ticket aspect. I will come back to this critical matter at a later stage when I have tilted a lance at some of the more technical aspects of education.

I do not like the pace of education. I cannot believe that the best use is now being made of the first 20 years of life. In my own experience I received 4 years of useful education over the whole period from the age of 4 to 21. I had a valuable year from my mother between 4 and 5, another such year when I first went to what you call junior high at the age of 11, then a good year in senior high between 17 and 18, and finally a good one at the university from 20 to 21. I am not saying the remaining years were entirely wasted, but that instruction was either muddled or hopelessly too slow. I have never heard any very serious discussion of what things a young child can be expected to learn well. Education seems to be predicated on the assumption that children start off as idiots and that as they grow older a rising tide of rationality gradually asserts itself. In some things at least this point of view is demonstrably false. Very occasionally it is found possible to restore the sight of an adult who has been unfortunate enough to be born blind. In such cases it is found that, although the optical qualities of the eye may work quite satisfactorily, sight in our common everyday sense is not automatically there. It is necessary to learn to see, and adults appear to find the learning process difficult or even impossible. A baby succeeds in solving this problem in the first 6 months of its life.

Nowadays speculations arise about the possibility of the human species on this planet managing to get in communication with creatures living on different planets moving around quite different stars from the Sun. One of the questions invariably asked is: How should we decipher each other's languages? You receive a stream of signals in some complicated code, and somehow you have got to crack that code. Well, this is exactly what babies succeed in doing in regard to language. When you already know one language, learning another is really a quite trifling matter, although we find it hard enough in all conscience. What a baby manages to do is the vastly more difficult job of cracking the basic code of language.

This leads me to one of the technical errors in our system of education. Very young children find the learning of languages absurdly easy. Why wait until the age of 11, by which time a child has already lost its linguistic abilities, before starting it on foreign languages? I remember staying with an English family in Germany shortly after the war. Both parents spoke good quality university German, which was far more than I did, but which was inferior to the German spoken by 80 million or so native speakers. The boy of 8 did better, but it was the younger boy of $2\frac{1}{2}$ who was the expert. He was quite indistinguishable from the native speakers.

Here we have an interesting social hiatus and the problem is to know how to jump over it. If once our societies were multilingual it would be easy for the different relatives of a young child to speak different languages to it. But how do you get started on such a system? Clearly, if different languages are to be spoken in the world, this is the way that learning should proceed. It is pointless starting when the ability has already gone. Schools should simply be used as conversation classes, so that children do not lose the languages they have already learned.

I suspect the situation to be somewhat similar in mathematics. There is a good deal of evidence to show that mathematical ability appears early in life. A story is told of the young Gauss, the famous German mathematician of the nineteenth century, when as a country boy he was admitted two years before his time to an advanced class in arithmetic at a town school. In the first lesson of the year the schoolmaster asked the boys to add up a set of numbers, as it happened spaced by a constant interval. Suppose you are asked to add up all the numbers from 1 to 100. You could proceed as follows: take the least number, 1, and add it to the highest number, 100, and together you get 101. Then take the next least number, 2, and add it to the next highest number, 99, and again you get 101. Now you started with 100 numbers in total so there must be 50 pairs, each adding up to 101, so the total is just 50 × 101, namely 5,050. The problem that Gauss's class was set by the teacher was similar to this, but harder. The young boy saw instantly how to solve the problem, wrote the answer as a single number on his slate, strolled to the front of the class, threw down the slate and said: "Well, that's that." The master took the young peasant boy for an idiot, glowered at him for a whole hour while the other boys slaved on the problem, obviously intending to beat the daylights out of him at the end of the hour. As Gauss said after in life, his was the only correct answer. The same boy succeeded a year or two later, in his early teens, in giving the first correct proof of Newton's famous binomial theorem. Of course this is not a typical case; Gauss was one of the finest mathematicians who has ever lived. But one case should be sufficient to convince us that children, even young children, are not necessarily intellectual dopes, as is undoubtedly predicated in our educational system. As I say, it is undoubtedly true that not every child possesses the mathematical ability of a Gauss, or even of a tenth of a Gauss, and it is true that experience—getting used to the tricks of the trade—is a help. But I doubt whether anyone is going to show useful mathematical ability in the late teens or twenties who has not already shown it at a much earlier age. If a child does possess mathematical ability it should be treated with respect, the same sort of respect that we show to a good student at the university. Instead we tend to despise such a child, I suspect largely because it is physically weak and because it has not learned a few routine tricks, such as the one I described above for adding up the numbers from 1 to 100.

It seems to me that our educational system proceeds on an utterly and completely wrong notion that the intellectual quality of what is taught should be correlated closely with age. I have chosen mathematics as an example, but the same thing applies to other disciplines. But to continue with mathematics, the present system is wrong because it asks for too little from young children who happen to be mathematically inclined, whereas it asks too much from older students who are not mathematically inclined. I can see no point at all in forcing those who have not the trick of mathematical argument to acquire certain specified standards in the later teens.

There is no particular virtue, moral virtue, in being able to understand mathematics; the reason why we talk about it so much is simply because it happens to be the gateway to the sciences. The trouble with the present system is that it holds back, very severely I suspect, whose who do have the trick of it, and it becomes a torture and a destroyer of self-confidence for those who have not. The situation is as absurd as if we demanded that all children run the hundred yards in under 11 seconds, whipping and flogging those who were unable to succeed, even after repeated, desperate, futile attempts. Nothing in education should be allowed to rob a child of self-confidence, especially if there is some one activity that the child happens to be particularly good at. It is on their strong points that children should be encouraged, not on the weak, for in their nature the weak subjects will never come to anything.

Then again there are some subjects that are taught too soon. Because of the biological processes that set in, in the early teens, a real change does take place in all of us. Certain subjects, particularly the humanities, are profoundly affected by these changes. I do not think a young child can be expected to understand anything of history. It simply does not possess the correct emotional structure to understand the motivations of adults. For many of us the plays of Shakespeare, deeply concerned as they are with the motives of love, hate, and power, were utterly incomprehensible at the age of 10 or 11. Yet we were meaninglessly exposed to them at that age and came to regard them as drivel, inferior to the activities of Superman. The point I am making that while a young child's logical faculties may be quite sophisticated, even by adult standards, its emotional judgment is, as we say, puerile. It is precisely because of this that a logically sophisticated child must not be moved out of a childhood environment. It is no solution to pack such a child off to the university. Children must play with children. The best conceivable lesson for an able child, when it first begins to value its abilities and gets a little smug about them, is to have its eyes blacked by the other kids.

But all this is by the way, since my main concern is with the late stages of education. I will be concerned far more with the late stages of university education in the sciences and mathematics than with the arts and humanities, simply because my own experience is in science and mathematics. It is an inevitable consequence of the fact that our students were taught far too little when they were young that they must be taught far too much as they come toward the age of 20. The position here I suspect is better in the United States than it is in Britain. My own university, Cambridge, is said to take the cream of the mathematical talent of the whole British Isles. This means I suppose that we get from one-third to one-half of the best mathematical talent of the United Kingdom. Our annual intake in mathematics is about 150 students. So we are working basically on the best 300–500 students out of a population of 50 million people. Yet the teaching we give is far too difficult for almost all students, only about 10 out of each year's crop manage to survive unharmed. Manifestly this is absurd, and the whole world realizes it except those who happen to be doing the teaching.

It is true that in other subjects and in other universities the same absurd lengths have not been reached. But the situation everywhere is somewhat similar in kind if not in degree. This is because universities today are serving a double function, a double function arrived at by the accidents of history, rather than by the logic of the present situation. In the past, students at the university fell into one or the other of two groups. There were the sons of the wealthy who attended for social reasons, and there was the professional scholar. If you were in the first category you did not study at all, or nearly not at all. If you were in the second you studied at a thoroughly professional level. And this of course is what the training in mathematics at Cambridge is to this day, a thorough training for professionals. It is exactly what the very ablest students need, not what is needed by an educational institution that has become a component of popular democracy. The same thing shows itself in the current confusion between education and research. The two are forced together in an uneasy marriage in our universities. The reason, I think, is that practical arguments of expediency can be found for the connection. But the point I have been leading up to is that no real intellectual connection exists at all between education and research.

The usual argument for the connection is that research is in constant need of new recruits, who come naturally from young graduates at the universities. At the same time it is pointed out that the appearance in the classroom of the active research worker is a stimulus to teaching. The second argument is somewhat specious, for the appearance in the classroom of the gifted research worker is only too likely to lift standards to impossible levels, as I have just pointed out. What is true, however, is that research does need a continuous supply of new recruits. And there is more to this than meets the eye, for I mean new recruits, not at all in the sense of cannon fodder but as a crowd of awkward customers who are able and willing to chalk off an established professor when he is wrong. A young recruit to business must kowtow to his boss, but the young recruit to research must do the opposite, at any rate he must be willing to do the opposite if he feels he is in the right. The iconoclasm of the young is essential if research is to keep healthy, and it so happens that no one has yet discovered a human organization that permits the young to be openly critical of the old except the university. Probably this is due to the fact that there are so many more young people on a university campus than there are old.

It may well be that this alone is a sufficient factor to prevent the main centers of research from ever being separated from the universities. But if this is to be so it is essential that the whole balance of education and research should be thought through. Education represents continuity. We are passing on the culture and technology of the human species from one generation to another, as the culture and technology exists at this particular moment. This is a big enough thing, it represents the whole accumulated experience of our species. It represents what we are. But research is something different. It is a probing toward things that are new, that we do not know at the moment. It represents the flashes I spoke of in a previous chapter, the mutations that in the past have produced our present knowledge and experience. Research is what will make the future.

Not only are the intellectual natures of education and research different in themselves, but the very faculties needed in their study are different. You will learn best, in an educational sense, if you believe exactly what you are told by your teachers. You would come to nothing at all in research if you believed what you were told, because by definition when your colleagues or teachers have failed to solve a problem it is because they are wrong, because they have got the wrong approach. And the motives underlying education and research are also different. We have seen that the forces impelling education are social, connected with the economic well-being of the individual and of society in general. The motives of the research worker had better have very little to do with this, although I fear only too often that they do. But the best attitude toward research is undoubtedly that of a wholly disinterested inquiry, the sort of inquiry that a young child has before it goes to school.

The tragedy of the present situation is that the interests and the need for research are very largely being overlooked in the current educational boom. As universities are expanding, so are research facilities, but for wrong and dangerous reasons. The attitude current in all universities so far as I can see, whether in the United States or in Europe, is that research facilities are provided as a spoonful of jam to the patient after he has swallowed the medicine of education. It is wrong to connect the two activities in this way. It is wrong to suggest that research activities are a kind of *quid pro quo* for services rendered in the field of education. Education is important in its own right, as I have shown. Research is utterly essential if the whole human species is not to fossilize at its present position. Both have strong claims on society and should receive independent treatment. The dangerous feature of the current situation is that research is being encouraged to swing along on the coattails of education. There is strong pressure on governments, of a social kind, to increase educational facilities —and so there should be. And the lazy man's method, which is usually the method that our societies elect to follow, is to ignore the problem of research, for which there is no very great popular vote, and to allow research to be carried along by the surging momentum of education.

The dangers in this to the universities are obvious. More and more, research facilities will become available outside the universities. This is already happening in parts of physics. High energy physics has become such an expensive pursuit that it will soon lie outside the financial range of any individual university. While it is true that a consortium of universities may agree together to support some combined facility, as is actually the case at Brookhaven, such facilities will gradually become independent organizations. As more and more such organizations become established and as research becomes increasingly subservient to education in the universities themselves, the ablest research workers will inevitably move out of the universities. Why stay in a place where the dice are loaded against you? So it could come about that within a short space of two or three decades the whole character of our universities will change. They will become exactly what they are at present aiming to become—educational institutions, not centers of learning and research.

It may turn out that there is nothing wrong in this, that universities will continue to flourish as centers of education and that independent organizations will flourish as centers of research. But I think we must hesitate a little before plunging blindly in this direction. We must always be cautious of throwing away an old system which has worked well in the past in favor of a new system. When the old system begins to go wrong, petty resistance to necessary modifications often forces a new system on us. Frequently in such cases it would have been much better to have admitted the modifications required to bring the old system into consonance with the current situation. I therefore wish to end the present chapter by suggesting that universities and governments give more attention than they have heretofore to the independent claims of research. There are no large blocks of votes to be won in elections from this. But the long-term prosperity and security of a nation depends on its research, and perhaps more on research, disinterested research, than on any other factor. In my last chapter I am going to maintain an even stronger position than this on the subject of research. I am going to ask what the human species lives for, what in the last analysis do you and I think we are doing here on the Earth? Is there any very much better answer than to attempt to decipher the great play that constitutes the Universe? This is the case for research. It is, I suggest, a case that demands respect —and attention.

CHAPTER FIVE

The Poetry of Earth
Is Never Dead

Keats when he wrote the words "The poetry of Earth is never dead" lived in a more placid, more contented, society than we do today. If he had been given a glimpse of our modern ant heap, with its appalling noise, traffic on the roads, congestion, and crowding, I wonder if he would still have made the same assertion. Nowadays people are even questioning whether the whole of life might not be utterly wiped out by a nuclear catastrophe, even the Earth might become dead, let alone its poetry. But this is a more depressing view than I hold myself. I do not think life will die on the Earth, but the poetry of life, which Keats perceived, seems to me to be under severe threat. In this final chapter I want to consider basic problems of motivation.

What do we think we are doing, here on the Earth?
I do not mean what do we think we are doing as indi-

viduals. I know what I am doing, and I am sure you know what you are doing.

I mean what do we think we are doing as a whole, as a species? Little effort is made in our everyday life to even consider this question, let alone to answer it. We are all so much concerned with the welfare of those immediately surrounding us that it is hard to focus at all on the larger issue. In an earlier chapter I spoke of our curious mixture of nearsightedness and farsightedness. Nearsightedness holds the field for such a major portion of our time—thinking about advancement in our jobs, thinking about next weekend, about our next vacation or our last vacation, about how the kids are doing—that we have little time or breath left for farsightedness. Yet it is clear that when roused we are capable of leaving aside everyday problems and of thinking about wider horizons.

The only time in my life when I have observed a large number of people really single-minded about a particular objective was, sadly to say, during the war. Probably not many people would be willing to accept the melancholy fact that the years of the war were in a certain sense the most satisfactory years of their lives. Yet I suspect that many feel the national determination and purpose of wartime to be preferable to the stumbling uncertainties of peacetime. Notice that I am arguing not that war is preferable to peace but that purposive action by a whole community is more stimulating to the individual than are vague uncertainties. The individual finds it difficult to give his best if the community around him has no directed motivation. Attempting to work in an aimless society is like living with a wet collar 'round your neck all the time.

Manifestly the great periods of individual achievement are correlated with the morale of communities. Great men arise whenever the communal attitude is one of confidence and purpose. The mere thought that in some other people, nation, or city the atmosphere is infinitely more favorable to what we are struggling to achieve is sufficient to discourage initiative and to damp out the creative fires. In every country, able men in all walks of life feel it necessary to hie themselves off to the main center of the stream of their own interest. It is not so easy in isolation to feel encouraged to write great music or great literature or good science. The conviction that another place is better for working than where we happen to be is quite sufficient to rob us of our inner confidence.

There is a real problem concerning morale. To be effective our sense of confidence must be soundly based. The world is full of countries, institutions, families that maintain a pretense of preeminence, when in fact their great days belong very definitely to the past. In such cases memories of former glory strangely impede all attempts at change, the pattern is rigid and decline is inevitable.

I find it an interesting thought that a community can have very much what it wants from the individuals that constitute it, provided only that the appropriate social environment be created. But this is not easy to do in any planned way. In the past, favorable environments have come about essentially by chance. The painters of Florence, the Elizabethan dramatists, the musicians of Vienna, all flourished for a brief while and then disappeared as the environments which produced them declined and withered away. Similarly, our present-day society, favorable to science and technology, could change, and science could decay, just as surely as did the civilizations of Greece and Rome. What I am saying is that leaving things to chance is not enough.

Only if we develop a clear understanding of the relationship between the individual and the community, only if we really understand our present-day situation, can we make plans for worthwhile activities to continue in the future.

To what extent can we say that such plans do exist? In some directions we are manifestly better placed than we were in the past. In the economic field, we are no longer obliged to submit to alternating boom and slump—it is probable that no depression like that of 35 years ago can occur nowadays, because ways of preventing it are understood. The symptoms of economic instability are understood and as soon as they show themselves governments take purposive action. Manifestly, however, what applies in the economic field is quite exceptional. As soon as we come to the international field we find nothing but muddle. The muddle is so appalling that even when an apparently progressive step is taken—such as the establishment of the United Nations—very little is achieved. The abominable situation in the Congo is an example of this ineffectiveness. What it comes down to is that mankind as a whole just does not know how to organize itself on the biggest scale of all. We know how to organize the workings of a city, even one so large as New York. More or less we know, by a long process of trial and error, how a nation can be organized—and this by the way is no mean feat. But so far we have no grip on the international scene. When I look at the details of everyday happenings I find myself wondering why the devil they do not do something sensible? I used to say exactly the same thing 35 years ago in the Depression. Since then, however, I have learned that doing something sensible is not easy. I used to think that only fools or knaves could have produced an economic situation with millions unemployed, millions lacking even the necessities of life, when if they were employed prosperity would be possible—an obvious feedback loop. Now I realize that clearing up the mess in the world would be a fantastically difficult problem, even if one were permitted to control the whole operation. What would you do if you were given the job of setting things to rights? Notice that you would be in a far more favorable position than the President of the United States, who can only exercise actual *control* here and who must proceed by *persuasion* on the international stage. But suppose you were not handicapped in this way, suppose you were in the driver's seat. What would you do?

I do not regard this as a fanciful question. It represents a procedure that is often used very fruitfully in science, argument from an idealized experiment, not from an actual experiment. Unless we are able to give a good answer, then plainly we cannot blame political leaders for making a botch of things. And unless a good answer is possible we can hardly expect the world to evolve, except by trial and error, in other words by the kind of biological evolution that I described in my second chapter.

The old-style answer was that good will would solve everything. At the Christmas season we receive the Christian exhortation that we should show "good will toward all men." I do not know whether it is because the Christian religion has already done such a good job or because we are all in the main fundamentally decent people, but good will does not seem to me to be a commodity that is in any way in short supply. I am convinced that if representatives at the United Nations knew how to make a better world they would do so. The trouble is that food has to be grown and distributed, goods manufactured and distributed, and these requirements immediately plunge us into technology and economics. It is here that we run into difficult problems, particularly of course the problem that only a minor proportion of the world's population is technology-oriented. At first sight the problem in the Congo might seem one of sheer animal savagery, but really I suspect the root of the matter to lie in the soils of Africa, in the lack of organic content in the soils. In my second chapter I pointed out that the evolution of mammals may have been contingent on the appearance of grass on this planet. Similarly, the development of civilization in Africa may turn on the emotionally negligible, but technically difficult, problem of soil composition. Indeed I suspect that we have here an example of a general truth, namely that human behavior is determined by the physical environment: an appropriate environment leads to civilization and to the concept of "good will toward mankind," a bad environment leads to animal savagery. If this is correct, then nothing can be achieved anywhere on the Earth at any time, except through the creation of the appropriate environmental conditions.

I have referred to scientific procedure in connection with the concept of the idealized experiment. The more direct method of actual experiment is difficult to adopt on a world-wide stage, and it is just here that a great deal of our trouble lies. The physicist or chemist does not usually have to worry too much if an experiment should fail, but failure in a major sociological experiment must affect the well-being, even the lives, of many millions. The situation is closer to the dilemma of the surgeon: should he experiment the life of his patient will be in balance, yet if he were never to experiment there could be no improvement in surgical methods. Plainly experiments cannot be carried out in the spirit of "let's try everything," as they can to a considerable extent in the inorganic sciences. We have to proceed responsibly, and the issue evidently boils down to how we are to define a *responsible* procedure. Such a procedure must bear a close relation to previous experience, and to the ideas we have developed from that experience, to what in science we would call *theory*.

In astronomy, we have a state of affairs somewhat similar in its tangled complexity to our problems on the human stage. We are faced by contradictions. Not all the apparent data of the moment can be correct. We do not know what fragments of data are right and what are wrong. Are some of the galaxies that we observe young or not? Because we cannot experiment with the universe, we live in a kind of shifting uncertainty, shifting because as the years pass the balance of certainty of a given piece of data changes. On the other hand, the precision of physical experiments causes physicists *at any moment* to assume an attitude of certainty. Yet physicists as a group change their views violently from generation to generation, quite as much as astronomers change theirs! Physics is analogous to a fracture of material which bears stress up to a certain point and which then gives way suddenly, as in an earthquake. Astronomy is more like plastic flow, and is therefore more akin to human affairs. The difference evidently lies in procedure, particularly experimental procedure.

In a complex and uncertain situation, when I have no

idea of the correct route, I like to follow an axiomatic kind of approach. I choose some noteworthy starting point, assume the starting point to be correct and proceed to argue deductively from there. Instead of attaching probabilities to the various facets of the situation and of then seeking the apparently best balanced description, I attribute unit probability, *certainly*, to my starting point, and then accept all the consequences that flow from deductive argument. Inevitably, fierce clashes between one's deductions and former beliefs, or apparent facts, will arise. Often these clashes are so bad that wisdom dictates that the whole thing be scrapped and that a new starting point be sought. But occasionally one comes up with something really interesting, and which is worth putting forward seriously, even though it may clash with some established ideas. The critical factor in such a method lies of course in the choice of starting position. We refer to scientists who choose their positions shrewdly as having "good physical intuition." Choices at random, in essence the method advocated many years ago by Descartes, have the disadvantage that the overwhelming proportion of your deductive work will be fruitless. Indeed, you may well run through the whole of your working life without hitting anything worthwhile.

Can the same procedure be adopted in our human problem? Is there a starting point that we could all agree to adopt from which everything else would follow by straightforward deduction, more or less as night follows day? In the past I have always felt that such a starting point could be found on the basis of cold logic, exactly as in a scientific problem. It seemed clear to me that the problem of world organization must be incapable of solution so long as elementary technological and arithmetical issues are made subservient to emotion. The soils of Africa are a technological example, the present startling rise of the world's population is an arithmetic example. Yet this does not seem the correct starting point, except perhaps to the one person in ten who has learned to make emotion subservient to logic, at any rate in the degree demanded by these questions. The difficulty is that when logic and emotion clash, as they must do in this case, logic is usually the casualty.

So it is essential to start from a position capable of withstanding all subsequent emotional storms. Suppose we take the position that we will no longer tolerate the majority of children being born into a world of misery and hunger. Suppose we take this as our number one axiom. Suppose we argue from this axiom with relentless logic, and suppose we agree that any other issue we find clashing with it, contradicting it, must go to the wall. What then? Immediately we see that standards must be lifted in underdeveloped countries, not as a matter of charity, but as our number one priority, even before "defense" if need be. Since it is a matter of simple arithmetic that too many children would make our objective impossible, it is clear that strict population control must be imposed. If you happen to be a Catholic and hold strong emotional views on population control, those views must go to the wall—otherwise you are not driving through the deductive logic, you are accepting a manifest contradiction. If this raises a crisis within you, concerning the relation of the soul and body, the crisis must be resolved by discarding your strongly held former beliefs about the soul. These are the considerations that inevitably flow from the primary position that children must not be born into agony and misery.

Since I am touching on a religious question, I will borrow a religious concept, and say that the devil's greatest success to date has been to persuade us that irreconcilables can somehow be reconciled. In the present case we all know it to be grossly wrong that the world should be organized in such a way that it simply is not fit for a child to be born into it. I am not speaking now of an American child or a European child, but of an average child, one who will know little of anything beyond disease, ignorance, and hunger. We all deplore this situation, and, other things being equal, we would be heartily glad to have it changed. Where the rub comes is that we cannot have it changed so long as we stick to other things we would like to believe, for instance to believe in the overriding importance of the soul.

So I would conclude that the first priority in dealing with the present chaos in the world is to decide which of our beliefs are irreconcilable with each other. After this has been sorted out with real clarity, a decision on what should be given first priority would not, I think, be very

difficult to arrive at. Indeed I have a better regard for my
fellow men than to suppose they would prefer narrow
self-interest to the kind of issue I have been putting before you. I suspect that if only the issues, the contradictions, could be exposed it would be possible even to win
an election for a policy along the lines I have been suggesting. Once it began to roll, in an emotional sense, I do
not think any other factors could stand in its way. The
ground has not yet been cleared for this to happen, we
are still living with irreconcilables, vaguely hoping that
things will somehow come all right: that we will manage
to muddle through without being forced to discard any
of our cherished beliefs. During the next two decades I
expect these issues to come into increasingly clear focus,
however, and I suspect they will become major political
issues well before the end of the century.

In the last part of this chapter I would like to look still
further ahead. I would like to express the hope that 30
years from now people will look back on the present day
with the same feeling that we look back on the years of
the Depression. Just as we have conquered the economic
problems that plagued our fathers, I would hope that as
the twenty-first century opens, the present muddles of
world organization might be on their way to solution.
What next? Perhaps a higher and higher standard of living for everybody. More machines at everybody's dis-
posal, more travel, more motion—a higher temperature
all round. One need only mention such possibilities to see
two things: that this would indeed be a popular aim and

that it would not prove an ultimately satisfactory goal for the human species. There would be nothing of the sense of purpose which I described earlier. There would be nothing but a meaningless and incoherent scramble, we should have a civilization that had degenerated into what one might describe as "biological noise," we should have a negation of the quotation I chose for the title of this chapter, for the poetry of Earth would then indeed be dead.

So long as something clear and explicit remains to be done, it is clear that a cooperative sense of purpose can be found without much difficulty. But what after the purpose has been achieved? There would of course still be the problem of "defending" ourselves. But when you can kill everybody on Earth many times over, the concept of defense becomes distinctly artificial. I often wonder whether societies do not whip up issues quite artificially in order to give themselves a communal sense of purpose, and I wonder whether we might not be doing this even today in our attitude toward "defense." I do not see any long-term solution to the problem of purpose in this direction.

In the past, religion played a critical and important role in giving unity and stability to communities, nations, and even to international associations, notably the Holy Roman Empire. The purpose of life was to prepare yourself for an after-life in which you hoped to be accorded the kind of life which your more fortunate contemporaries were enjoying right now. The rising standard of life produced by the advance of technology, perhaps more than the technology itself, has utterly destroyed this sense of purpose. Nothing very much remains of the perquisites of the after-life except such things as "bliss," a word apparently intended to describe the indefinable. So we arrive at a not very enviable position. Both the material and spiritual aims of life are in retreat, and the human species looks as if it may become glutted by the very things it has always desired. The enemy is no longer the devil, and if technology is developed and applied, poverty need no longer be the enemy in the world of the future. Boredom, monotony, will then be our problems.

Luckily our most formidable opponent will remain, and will remain for any conceivable step into the future. Many physicists are hoping for an ultimate understanding of the laws of physics. But an ultimate understanding is most unlikely, since this would imply that our intellectual capabilities are rather precisely adjusted to the depth of subtlety of the basic laws. It might of course be so, but plainly any such matching of our brains to the external world would be an extreme fluke. Rather does it seem as if the Universe may have the aspect of completeness at all stages of sophistication. At every stage of scientific development it seems as if the final truth lies just around the next corner. The Greeks believed this to be the case, so did the eighteenth century and the nineteenth century, and now the twentieth century has the same notion. I suspect that it will prove just as illusory as before. The important thing about our perception of Nature is that by the time we realize a problem exists we are already well on the way to its solution. We are shielded from the problems we would have no hope at all of solving, simply because we cannot conceive of them. Our concepts are built from the things we can understand, and they serve us very well at our particular level of sophistication. But they scarcely permit us even a glimpse of a more advanced stage of sophistication. This is as well, for otherwise we should soon become discouraged. I do not doubt that as long as human beings continue to inhabit this planet there will be more things to be discovered, more problems to be solved. In this sense indeed the poetry of the Earth will never die.

In the second chapter I said that the laws of physics, the laws which prescribe the "game," represent the modern extrapolation of the concept of God. Now I would like to suggest that the further investigation of the game, the further digging to deeper levels of understanding, will be the only really long-range motivation that our species will ever find. We have a similar situation to the balance between chemistry and electronics, which I also described in the second chapter. You may remember that in the course of biological evolution it seems that an inversion of importance has occurred—at first we have electronics subservient to chemistry, but at a later stage the chemistry of the body becomes the servant of the brain. And in the first stage of human development our interest in problems has undoubtedly been directed toward biological survival. It must still be so directed, if the whole world is to be lifted out of its present mess. There is still some distance to go before the material requirements of the whole species are satisfied. Yet not very far ahead of us in time there must come an inversion of importance, when we exercise our curiosity about the world, about its structure and its laws, simply for their own sake. Today we are living close to a critical dividing point in the long-term history of our species. Yesterday, it was as much as we could do to survive and even our abstract curiosity had to be turned to material advantage. Tomorrow, our material requirements will be satisfied and abstract curiosity must stand in its own right if we are to survive as a species with purpose.

A radical and critical change, such as I am now proposing, is not likely to come about without our passing through a period of maladjustment. We can see evidence of maladjustment in the most developed countries. It shows in our incessant concentration on machines. Machines have hitherto played an essential role in freeing us from misery and want. Now that the developed countries are so freed, we are momentarily nonplussed. All we can think of is to go on making more and more machines, for their own sake it seems. We hardly seem to realize that the end of the road has been reached and that there is very little more that prosperous nations stand to gain from the machine age.

Even in research, the machine age is running riot. While it is true that no human being can think straight without a constant diet of facts, and that facts demand experiments, and experiments demand machines, this is no defense against the charge that we are absurdly biased in favor of machines and against abstract thought. The first question you will be asked if you make a new research proposal is very likely: Does it have any use? What is meant by use? A useful idea is simply one that serves to make machines. And the most useful idea is the one that serves to make the most machines, the more machines the more the use.

As I say, we are living in an age of changing values. For the moment we are bamboozled by technology, dead-drunk with it. But sooner or later society must waken and realize that nothing in the long run is to be gained from the present roaring commotion. It must come to see that the highest order of things lies in perception, in understanding the universal game that is going on around us, the game of which we are perhaps a tiny part. This is our future. I would claim it to be the only future, the only purpose, in which we as a species will find any ultimate long-term satisfaction.